A-Z
Animal Facts
For Kids

Contents

Ardvark

🐾 African aardvarks are nocturnal creatures.

🐾 Aardvarks are actually related to elephants, despite their vast difference in physical appearance.

🐾 Aardvarks can weigh up to 200 pounds and reach lengths of up to six feet.

🐾 Aardvarks have huge ears, long nostrils, and a long, sticky tongue that they use to gather termites and ants.

🐾 Aardvarks can construct tunnels and burrows in the ground with their keen claws.

🐾 Aardvarks are solitary creatures that only assemble to mate.

- Aardvarks are herbivores that primarily eat termites and ants.

- Aardvarks have a top speed of 30 mph.

- Due to habitat damage and hunting, aardvarks are regarded as a vulnerable species.

- The only species of the phylum Tubulidentata that is still alive is the aardvark.

- Aardvarks are indigenous to Africa and are widespread across the continent.

- Aardvarks have long snouts that resemble those of pigs, which is why their digging behavior earned them the nickname "earth pig" in Afrikaans.

- Being nocturnal creatures, aardvarks are most active at night.

- Although aardvarks have limited vision, they have strong hearing and smelling senses.

- The typical lifespan of aardvarks in the wild is between 10 and 15 years.

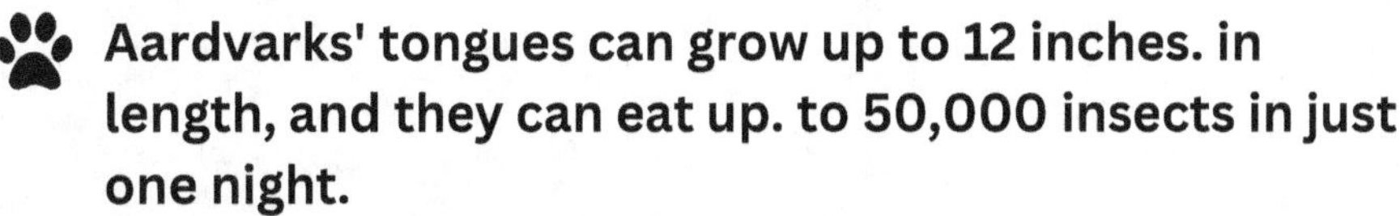 Aardvarks' tongues can grow up to 12 inches. in length, and they can eat up. to 50,000 insects in just one night.

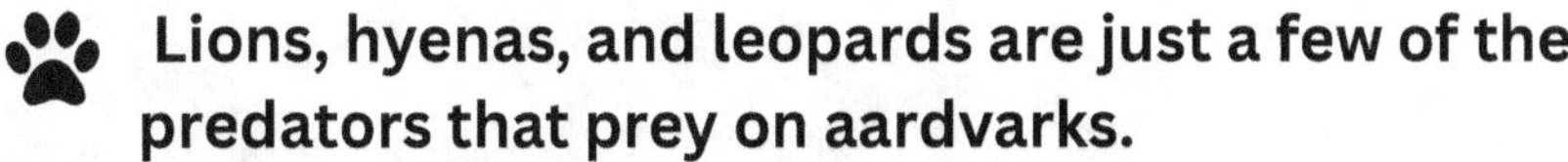 Lions, hyenas, and leopards are just a few of the predators that prey on aardvarks.

Aardvarks over the years have adapted to their environment by changing color to blend in with the soil.

Bear

- Bears are mammals, which means they have warm-blooded bodies, fur, and milk for nursing their young.

- With the exception of Antarctica, bears can be found in the wild everywhere.

- There are eight different species of bears around the globe, including the Grizzly Bear, the Panda Bear, the Sun Bear, the American Black Bear, and the Sloth Bear.

- Bears consume both vegetation and animals since they are omnivores.

- Bears' hearing and sense of smell are excellent, but their vision is poor.

- Bears rarely socialize with one another; they only do so when mating or when they are with their offspring.

- Bears can be fiercely competitive and will fight to protect their territory or food.

- In the wild, bears can live up to 30 years.

- Bears are excellent climbers and swimmers.

- To save energy, bears typically hibernate during the winter.

- Bears can outrun a racehorse over short distances thanks to their 40 mph top speed.

- Bears can spend up to seven months a year hibernating.

- Up to 18 miles away, bears can detect the fragrance of food.

- Bears can swim at a speed of up to 6 miles per hour.

- Polar bears can better absorb heat from the sun thanks to their dark skin and transparent fur.

- A unique muscle in grizzly bears enables them to extend their mouths wide enough to accommodate an entire fish.

- To gain a closer look at something, bears have been known to stand on their hind legs.

- A bear can pick up objects and even open jars with its front paws, which resemble human hands.

- Bears can recall where they left their food for up to a year and have a great memory.

- Little bears are known as "cubs," as they are born helpless and blind.

Cats

🐾 Cats are among the most widely owned pets in the world.

🐾 By licking their fur, they are excellent at keeping themselves clean.

🐾 Cats use their whiskers to aid with nighttime navigation.

🐾 Cats can jump up to five times higher than themselves.

🐾 Cats have been kept as pets for a very long time.

🐾 Cats can speak to people by meowing.

- Unlike other animals, cats have color vision.

- Cats live for 15 to 20 years on average.

- Cats must consume meat in order to thrive, making them obligate carnivores.

- There are 12 incisors, 10 premolars, 4 canines, and 4 molars among the 30 adult teeth that cats have.

- Cats can be left- or right-pawed, just like humans can be left- or right-handed.

- Cats knead with their paws when they're happy.

- Cats have nearly twice as many neurons in their cerebral cortex as dogs.

- Cats can jump up to five times their own height.

- A group of cats is called a clowder.

- Cats sometimes meow to initiate play, not just to communicate.

- Cats can fit through any opening the size of their head or larger.

🐾 Cats can hear ultrasonic sounds that humans can't.

🐾 Cats spend nearly one-third of their waking hours grooming themselves.

🐾 Cats sometimes purr when they're angry or in pain.

Dogs

🐾 One of the most well-liked pets in the world is the dog.

🐾 There are more than 340 different dog breeds.

🐾 The ability to smell is 100,000 times more acute in puppies than in us.

🐾 Dogs have greater night vision than people do.

🐾 Dogs use their tongues and noses to investigate the world around them.

🐾 Canines may be taught to detect bed bugs!

🐾 Dogs may be taught to spot human cancer!

🐾 Dogs have a unique way of using their tails to communicate!

🐾 Dogs are able to learn around 250 words!

🐾 Dogs are able to predict impending storms!

🐾 The Chihuahua is the world's tiniest dog breed, and the Irish Wolfhound is the tallest.

🐾 The Saluki, which dates back to ancient Egypt and was employed for desert hunting, is the oldest breed of domesticated dog that is now known.

🐾 Dogs like interacting with people and other canines since they are highly sociable creatures. They frequently wag their tails, lick their owners, or cuddle up to them as a way of expressing their love

🐾 The heart rate of a dog is twice that of a human.

🐾 Dogs live 10 to 13 years on average.

🐾 According to the American kennel club, the Labrador Retriever is the most popular dog in the united states

- Dogs have extraordinary hearing abilities and can distinguish sounds up to four times farther away than people.

- Dogs may be taught to perform incredible tasks like search and rescue, guiding the blind, and detecting hazardous materials.

- Dogs can make a variety of vocalisations, such as barking, howling, growling, whining, and occasionally even "talking." Individual dogs and dogs of different breeds each have their own distinctive vocalisations and ways of interacting with people and other animals.

Elephant

- The world's largest land animal is the elephant.

- Elephants' front feet have four toes, while their back feet have five.

- Elephants have two sets of teeth: their mouth's molars and their modified incisors, which are found on their tusks.

- Elephant pregnancies can last up to 22 months.

- Elephants have a daily dietary intake of up to 300 pounds.

- Elephants have a lifespan of up to 70 years.

- Elephants have great memories and are able to identify other elephants they have previously encountered.

- Elephants live in enormous groupings known as herds and have highly evolved social structures.

- Elephants are incapable of jumping!

- Elephants can spend up to six minutes underwater by using their trunks as snorkels.

- Elephants are the largest terrestrial creatures in the world. Adult males can weigh up to 5,500–6,600 kg (12,000–14,500 lbs) and can reach a shoulder height of 3.3 metres (11 feet).

- Elephants greet one another in a very special way by wrapping their trunks together!

- Newborn elephants can consume up to 50 liters of milk per day!

- Elephants are the only creatures having "trunks," which are actually the top lip and nose combined!

- 🐾 One of the rare animals that can recognize itself in a mirror is an elephant. This demonstrates that they are self-aware and are able to recognise themselves in the mirror.

- 🐾 An elephant's tusks can grow up to 10 feet long and never stop growing!

- 🐾 Of all land animals, elephants have the greatest brains. Their brain is around four times larger than the human brain and can weigh up to 5 kg.

- 🐾 Elephants make low-frequency rumbles that may be heard up to 6 kilometers apart from one another to communicate!

Fox

- 🐾 The canine family, which also contains wolves, dogs, and jackals, includes foxes.

- 🐾 Foxes are able to survive in the wild thanks to their strong senses of smell, hearing, and eyesight.

- 🐾 Foxes can be found in a range of hues, such as red, silver, grey, and black.

- 🐾 Fruits, insects, and small animals make up the food of foxes, who are omnivores.

- 🐾 Foxes construct their own burrows or dens to live in.

- Foxes are extremely sociable creatures that live in family or pack groups.

- Foxes are often referred to as "night hunters" because they are active at night.

- Foxes can leap up to three feet in the air and are great jumpers.

- Foxes use a range of sounds to communicate, including barks, whines and screams.

- Foxes can be found in a variety of environments, but they favor woodland places.

- When running and jumping, foxes use their long, bushy tails to assist them maintain balance.

- Foxes can jump more than two meters in a single bound!

- Foxes have extraordinary hearing and are able to detect the subsurface movement of small animals.

- Foxes are intelligent and have been known to learn how to unlock latches and doors.

- Foxes are capable of running at up to 25 mph!

- 🐾 Foxes can change their color from red in the summer to white in the winter, depending on the season.

- 🐾 Foxes enjoy playing and are frequently spotted playing tag with one another.

- 🐾 Foxes are capable of swimming and can submerge themselves for up to a minute.

- 🐾 One of the most adaptable mammals on the planet, foxes can live in a range of various environments, including cities, deserts, and woodlands.

- 🐾 Foxes are renowned for their intellect and aptitude for learning new things. They have been seen using tools, like flipping over stones with their paws to reveal food.

Gorilla

- Gorillas are among the most intelligent animals in the world and the largest of the apes.

- As gorillas are herbivores, they mostly consume plant materials including fruits, leaves, and stems.

- Gorillas can weigh up to 400 pounds and reach heights of up to 6 feet.

- A dominant male known as a silverback leads the army of gorillas.

- Gorillas talk to one another by grunting and growling.

- East and Central African rainforests are home to gorillas.

- In the wild, gorillas can live for up to 50 years.

- Gorillas can use tools to aid in nest building and food gathering.

- Gorillas can grasp objects more easily because they have opposable thumbs, just like humans.

- Due to habitat loss and poaching, gorillas are a threatened species.

- Gorillas can be pretty humorous! They can be seen interacting with one another in the wild and having fun.

- They are excellent climbers and can scale 60-foot trees.

- Although gorillas are vegetarians, they also enjoy eating termites.

- A troop refers to a group of gorillas.

- Like human fingerprints, gorillas have distinctive nose prints that can be used to identify individuals.

- 🐾 Gorillas are incredibly affectionate and have a tight bond with their young.

- 🐾 Mothers carry their babies on their backs for the first several months of their life, and they frequently cuddle and kiss their children.

- 🐾 Gorillas are among the most cognitive primates and have the ability to employ tools to resolve issues.

- 🐾 Gorillas can even pick up sign language and comprehend human speech!

Hedgehog

🐾 Nighttime creatures known as hedgehogs live throughout Europe, Asia, and Africa.

🐾 Hedgehogs can protect themselves from predators by using a spiky coat on their bodies.

🐾 To find food, hedgehogs utilize their snouts.

🐾 Being omnivores, hedgehogs consume fruits, vegetables, insects, small reptiles, and other zooplankton.

🐾 When threatened, hedgehogs wrap themselves into a ball.

- Hedgehogs have a top speed of 6 mph.

- The backs of hedgehogs have more than 6,000 spines.

- Hedgehogs have a maximum daily sleep time of 18 hours.

- Being nocturnal animals, hedgehogs are most active at night.

- A dog's sense of smell is up to 8 times better than a hedgehog's.

- Although they don't frequently do so, hedgehogs can climb trees.

- Insects, worms, and even little snakes and lizards are all consumed by hedgehogs.

- Sniffles, grunts, and squeals are just a few of the many sounds that hedgehogs can make.

- Hedgehogs can swim, but they don't particularly enjoy it.

- Hedgehogs have a two-foot vertical jump.

- 🐾 In the wild, hedgehogs can live up to 6 years, but in captivity, they can live up to 10 years.

- 🐾 Due to their role in maintaining the ecosystem's equilibrium, hedgehogs are regarded as an essential component of many ecosystems.

- 🐾 Hedgehogs are solitary creatures that prefer to live by themselves; they only assemble to breed.

- 🐾 Hedgehogs can socialize with humans, and certain species like the African Pygmy Hedgehog —have become well-liked pets.

- 🐾 Spines in hedgehogs are essentially modified hairs formed of keratin, the same substance found in human hair and nails.

Iguana

🐾 Huge lizards called iguanas inhabit tropical areas.

🐾 They can weigh more than 20 pounds and grow to be over 6 feet long.

🐾 Iguanas have long tails and scaly skin.

🐾 Iguanas mostly consume plants and fruit, making them herbivores.

🐾 They can defend themselves by using their powerful claws and pointed teeth.

- Iguanas blend in with their surroundings by using their color.

- Iguanas can swim, however, they normally hang out by the water's edge.

- Iguanas can see in color and have good eyesight.

- Iguana females dig burrows underground to lay their eggs.

- In captivity, iguanas can live up to 20 years.

- Due to their long tails and spiky skulls, iguanas are occasionally mistaken for dragons.

- Iguanas' colors can shift from brilliant green to deeper hues depending on how they're feeling.

- Iguanas have a light-sensitive area that functions as their third eye on top of their heads, which aids in detecting danger.

- To prevent loud noises, iguanas can cover their ears.

- Iguanas can submerge for up to 30 minutes!

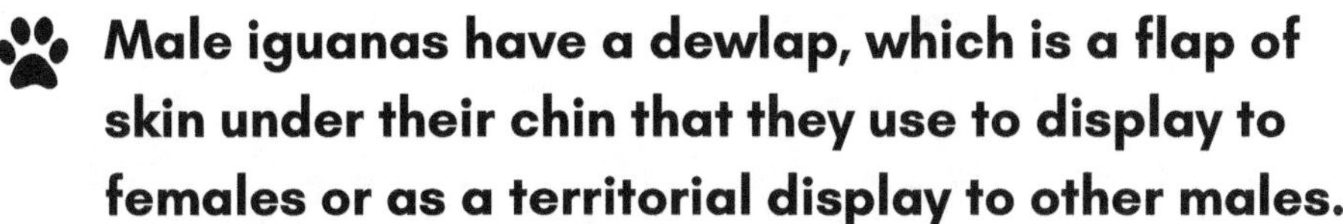 Male iguanas have a dewlap, which is a flap of skin under their chin that they use to display to females or as a territorial display to other males.

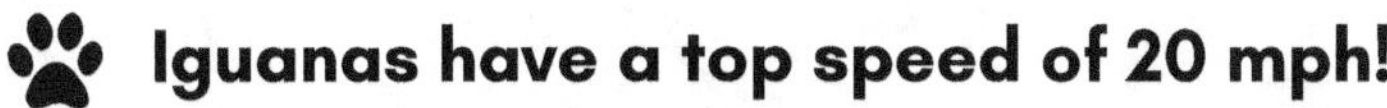 Iguanas have a top speed of 20 mph!

Iguanas have a 6-foot vertical jump capability!

Even iguanas can swim!

Iguanas are sometimes kept as pets.

Iguanas have a unique adaptation that allows them to regulate their body temperature. They bask in the sun to warm up, and they can change the color of their skin to absorb or reflect sunlight.

Jellyfish

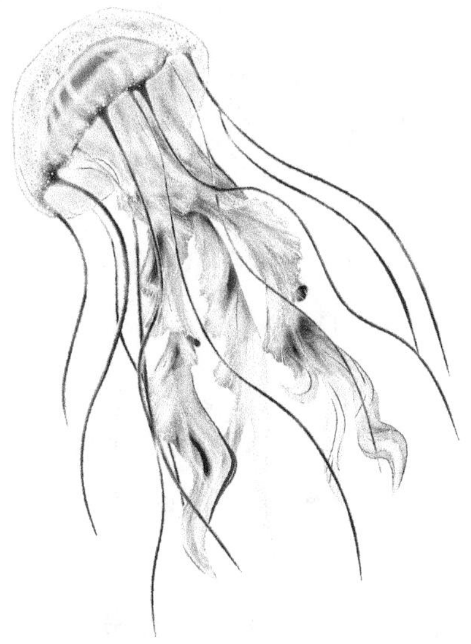

🐾 Jellyfish are invertebrates, not fish, which indicates they don't have a backbone.

🐾 From the surface to the deep water, jellyfish can be found throughout the world's oceans.

🐾 There are many different types of jellyfish, some of which can get as big as people while others can be as small as a fingernail.

🐾 Jellyfish have a distinctive jelly-like feel because they are 95 percent water.

🐾 Mesoglea, bell, oral arms, and tentacles are the four different body sections of jellyfish.

- 🐾 Despite having no brains or central nervous systems, jellyfish can feel their environment.

- 🐾 Depending on the species, jellyfish can act as both prey and predator.

- 🐾 Jellyfish are capable of reproduction on their own or with a mate.

- 🐾 Jellyfish are carnivores, which means they consume other marine life.

- 🐾 Some jellyfish have the ability to glow at night because they have unique proteins called photoproteins.

- 🐾 As jellyfish lack brains, they are unable to think or feel emotions.

- 🐾 Jellyfish come in a variety of hues, such as pink, blue, yellow, and purple.

- 🐾 In the wild, jellyfish can live for up to two years.

- 🐾 Jellyfish are soft and squishy because they lack bones.

- 🐾 Jellyfish move in a peculiar way. They move across the water by pulsing their umbrella-like bodies.

- One of the world's most dangerous organisms, the box jellyfish is primarily found in the waters of the Indo-Pacific. Its sting can be fatal to humans.

- The tentacles of jellyfish can reach a length of ten feet.

- Plankton, a small animal and plant, are consumed by jellyfish.

- There have been jellyfish on the planet for millions of years.

- Jellyfish are consumed in dishes like jellyfish salad in various regions of the world where they are regarded as delicacies.

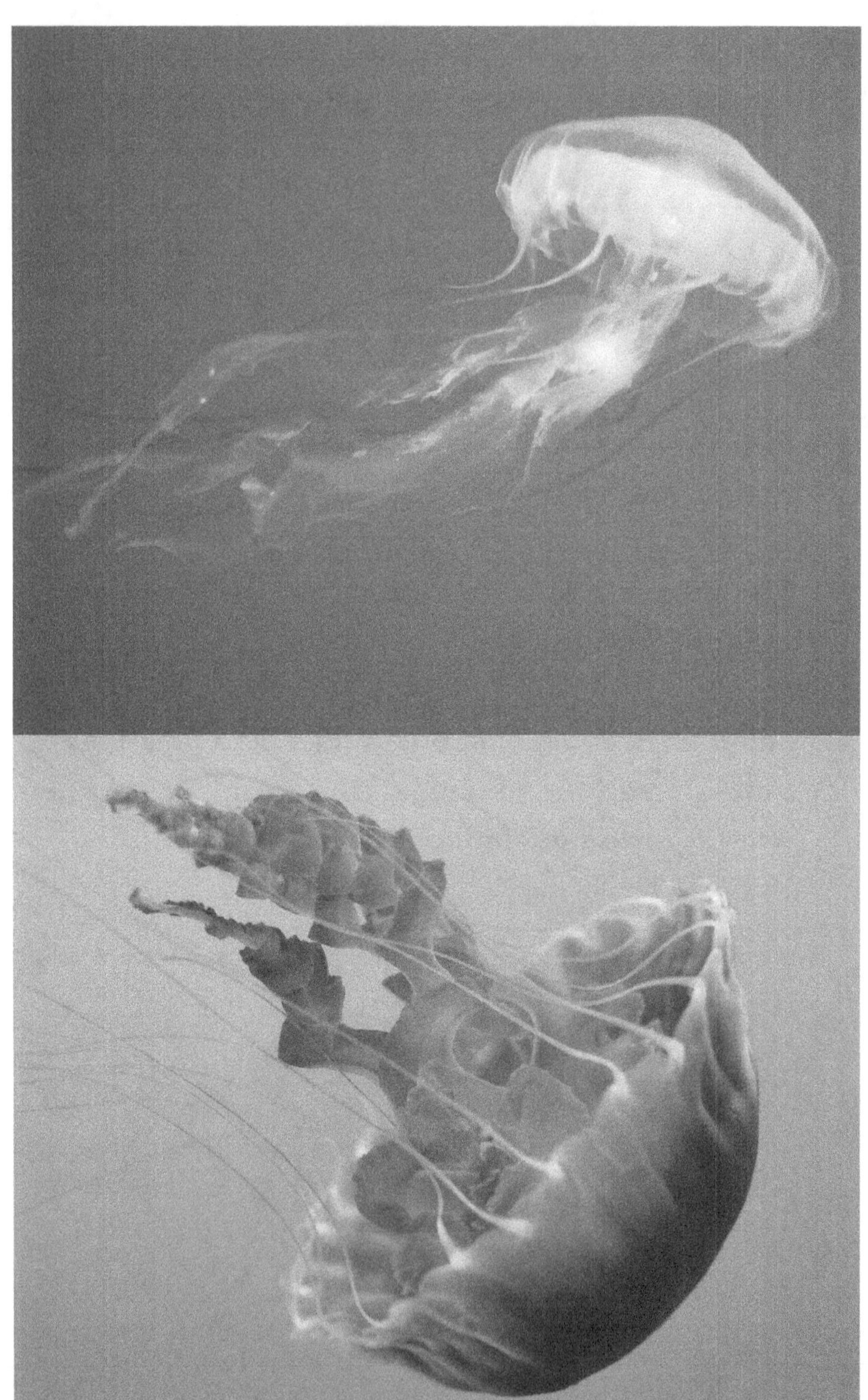

kangaroo

- Native to Australia, kangaroos are a subspecies of marsupial mammal.

- Kangaroos can jump up to 10 feet in a single bound.

- In hopping, kangaroos utilize their strong tails to balance and guide.

- Female kangaroos carry their offspring in pouches located on their tummies.

- A joey is the name given to a newborn kangaroo, which is often the size of a small bean.

- Being herbivores, kangaroos exclusively consume vegetation.

- Kangaroos have keen hearing and eyesight, which aid in their ability to identify predators.

- Being gregarious animals, kangaroos reside in big groups known as mobs.

- In the wild, kangaroos can live up to 20 years.

- The red kangaroo, which can grow to a height of 6 feet and weigh up to 200 pounds, is the largest species of kangaroo.

- To assist keep dust and other particles out of their eyes, kangaroos have three distinct eyelids.

- A female kangaroo is referred to as a flyer, whereas a male is referred to as a boomer.

- The red kangaroo, eastern grey kangaroo, western grey kangaroo, and antilopine kangaroo are the four species of kangaroos.

- Even though they can swim, kangaroos prefer to stay on land.

- Kangaroos have a top sprint speed of 40 mph.

- Kangaroos can leap obstacles that are twice as high as themselves.

- Australia's national animal, the kangaroo, is shown on its coat of arms.

- A kangaroo can kick with both legs simultaneously, and their kicks can be lethal to predators

- Australia's indigenous cultures place a high value on kangaroos, who are frequently depicted in both art and literature.

Lion

🐾 The only cats that live in communities known as a "pride" are lions.

🐾 Male lions have unique manes that surround their heads.

🐾 When running, lions are capable of reaching speeds of up to 81 km/h (50 mph).

🐾 After tigers, lions are the second-largest cats in the world.

🐾 Lions mostly consume meat, including antelope, zebra, and wildebeest.

- Lions in the wild can live up to 14 years.

- Lion cubs cannot see until they are around a month old as they are born blind.

- Lions can be found in portions of Asia and Africa.

- Lions are the national animals of Singapore, Belgium, England, Bulgaria, and Albania.

- Lions are the only cats that have the ability to roar.

- Lions roar to keep other lions away and to defend their territory.

- Lions may snooze for as much as 20 hours each day!

- Up to 8 km away, a lion's roar can be heard.

- A lion's tail can reach a length of one metre.

- A pride of lions, which can number up to 40, typically consists of connected females, their cubs, and a few males.

- The mane of a male lion can be up to one meter long.

- While running, lions can travel up to 81 km/h.

- Lions have a 3-meter vertical jump capability.

- Lions enjoy playing and fighting with one another!

- Lions are superb hunters who can take down game that is much bigger than themselves. They quickly suffocate and kill their victim by choking them with their strong jaws and pointed teeth.

Monkey

Monkeys are primates which are a class of mammals.

Tropical regions in Africa, Asia, Central America, and South America are home to monkeys.

Living in groups, monkeys are extremely sociable creatures.

Monkeys can communicate with one another by using facial expressions.

Monkey tails can grow to a length of three feet.

- The diets of various monkey species vary, and they may eat fruit, seeds, nuts, insects, small animals, and even some plants.

- To find food, monkeys utilize tools like sticks to dig for grubs.

- Due to their keen vision and hearing, monkeys are attentive and adept at spotting danger.

- In the wild, monkeys can live up to 45 years.

- Monkeys can peel bananas with their feet and like eating them!

- With their long arms and powerful hands, monkeys can swing from one tree to another.

- Monkeys have tails that assist them in maintaining balance while climbing.

- Because of their keen sense of smell, monkeys frequently detect objects from great distances.

- Monkeys dwell in large groups known as a troop.

- Monkeys like grooming one another by removing dirt and insects from one another's fur.

- To grab objects, monkeys use their tail as a second hand.

- With their calls and screeches, monkeys can create quite a bit of noise.

- In addition to playing practical jokes on one another, monkeys have been known to steal food from unwary tourists.

- Monkeys have a high level of intelligence and can even pick up tool use.

- Monkeys range in size from the tiny pygmy marmoset, at about 5 inches long, to the large mandrill, which can weigh up to 120 pounds.

Newt

🐾 Because newts are amphibians, they can exist both on land and in water.

🐾 The life cycle of a newt has three stages: egg, larva, and adult.

🐾 From dry forest areas to wetland settings, newts can be found in a variety of habitats.

🐾 In the wild, newts can live up to 15 years, and up to 20 years in captivity.

🐾 Because of their very toxic skin, newts should never be handled by people.

🐾 Worms and insects are among the tiny invertebrates that newts devour.

- Newts breathe through their skin.

- During the winter, newts hibernate.

- To defend themselves from predators, newts create toxins.

- Newts lay their eggs in the water after mating in the spring.

- Newts can grow back missing limbs like tails and toes.

- Newts are a type of Salamander

- Newts are also capable of changing their skin color to blend in with their environment.

- There are over 100 species of newts.

- Newts have an interesting courtship ritual, which involves the male performing a "dance" to impress the female.

- Newts have very poor eyesight, so they rely on their sense of smell and taste to find food.

- Australia and Antarctica are the only places in the world that don't have newts.

- Newts have four different types of eyelids: brille, nictitating membranes, and ordinary eyelids.

- To stay moist and shield themselves from predators, newts have slimy skin.

- Newts can be found in North America, Europe, and Asia.

- The way newts move while they walk is different. Newts lift their bellies off the ground while moving ahead with their legs.

Ostrich

- **With males weighing up to 320 lbs, ostriches are the largest species of living birds (145 kg).**

- **Ostriches are the fastest two-legged mammal, with a top speed of 43 mph (70 kph).**

- **With eyelashes that can reach 4 inches long, ostriches boast the longest feathers of any bird (10 cm).**

- **Ostriches can jump up to 9 feet (2.7 m) in the air, but they cannot fly.**

- **An ostrich can lay an egg that weighs up to 3 lbs, making them the largest egg-laying bird (1.4 kg).**

- The three stomachs that ostriches have makes it easier for them to digest their plant-based diet.

- Ostriches can dwell in flocks of up to 30 birds and are indigenous to Africa and the Middle East.

- Ostriches can push predators away because of their strong legs and long toes.

- Ostriches have sturdy, puffy feathers that keep them warm in cold weather.

- Being omnivores, ostriches consume seeds, plants, insects, and small animals.

- The only bird with genitalia is the ostrich!

- Compared to other terrestrial animals, ostriches have the largest eyes.

- In the wild, ostriches can live up to 75 years.

- Ostriches may produce eggs up to 7 inches long, the largest of any living bird.

- Unlike other birds, which have four toes on each foot, ostriches only have two.

- An ostrich may go four to five days without water.

- Ostriches have been observed to use their wings to blow a cloud of dust at an approaching predator, rendering it blind.

- When running, ostriches utilize their wings to aid with balance.

- Ostriches can go up to two weeks without eating.

- Ostriches have an unusual reproductive system in which the dominant male in the group incubates the eggs laid by the females in a communal nest.

Penguin

🐾 Penguins live in the southern hemisphere.

🐾 There are 18 different species of penguins, the tallest and heaviest of which is the Emperor penguin.

🐾 Penguins can be seen huddling together for warmth in their colonies.

🐾 Penguins can swim underwater at a pace of up to 15 mph by using their wings.

🐾 Penguins consume fish, squid, krill, and other oceanic crustaceans as food.

- Once a year, penguins molt, or shed their feathers.

- To remain warm in frigid areas, penguins have a coating of insulating feathers and blubber.

- To catch prey, penguins can leap up to six feet into the air.

- When a penguin lays an egg, the male typically keeps it warm for two months until the offspring hatch.

- Penguins play a crucial role in the food chain and support a healthy ocean ecology.

- While penguins cannot fly, they are skilled swimmers!

- Penguins have an additional feather covering that helps keep them warm and dry in chilly water.

- When walking, penguins waddle.

- The upper and lower eyelids of penguins enable them to see underwater.

- 🐾 Penguins can move swiftly across the water because to their webbed feet.

- 🐾 Penguins coat their feathers with a unique oil to help keep them waterproof.

- 🐾 In cold weather, penguins gather in groups to stay warm.

- 🐾 Penguins can submerge themselves for up to 20 minutes.

- 🐾 Male penguins give stones as gifts to their mate.

Quail

- Quails are small, ground-dwelling birds that can be found in a range of settings, such as grasslands, woodlands, deserts, and agricultural land.

- Quails can fly up to 20 miles per hour and are skilled pilots.

- Quails consume both vegetation and animals since they are omnivores.

- Quail nests are typically hidden in the grass or behind foliage, where the eggs are laid.

- Quails often dwell in small flocks, while some are able to live alone.

- Quails inhabit a variety of habitats, including grasslands, wooded areas, deserts, and agricultural land.

- There are numerous species of quails that can be found all over the world, including in North America, Europe, Asia, Africa, and Australia.

- Quails are sociable birds that reside in flocks or coveys, frequently made up of multiple pairs or families.

- Numerous kinds of quails are hunted for sport and their meat is regarded as a delicacy in various cultures, making them common game birds.

- Quails are capable of running at up to 10 mph!

- A clutch of quails can include up to 8 eggs!

- A variety of calls, such as the "cuckoo," are made by quails.

- Quails frequently appear in couples or compact groups known as "coteries."

- In comparison to their body size, quails have among of the longest legs among birds.

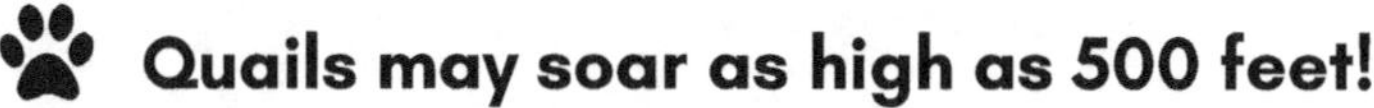

- 🐾 Quails may soar as high as 500 feet!

- 🐾 Up to ten years have been recorded for quails' lifespans!

- 🐾 Quails are so little that they could hide in your jeans' pockets!

- 🐾 To keep themselves clean and get rid of parasites, quails occasionally take dust baths!

- 🐾 When quails are content, they frequently purr!

Rabbit

🐾 Wild rabbits dwell in communities known as "warrens."

🐾 Rabbits prefer to live in groups and are gregarious creatures.

🐾 Rabbits are herbivores that solely consume plants.

🐾 To help them jump and run quickly, rabbits have long ears and large back legs.

🐾 While running, rabbits may reach up to 40 kph.

- Rabbits can look around them almost completely without turning their heads.

- To navigate in the dark, rabbits utilize their whiskers as a sense of touch.

- Rabbits have large teeth that keep growing longer as they age.

- Rabbits are born hairless, blind, and deaf.

- Young rabbits are referred to as "bunnies."

- With more than twice as many taste buds as humans, rabbits have around 2,000!

- Rabbits have a 3-foot vertical jump capability!

- Rabbits can have ears that are up to 4 inches long!

- Rabbits have a ten-year lifespan!

- Rabbits are prolific breeders; they can have up to 12 litters of young per year and are renowned for their quick reproduction.

 Rabbits will consume their own waste!

 Rabbits never stop growing and have 28 teeth.

Rabbits' ears can turn 180 degrees!

Rabbits enjoy eating lettuce, hay, and other vegetables in addition to carrots.

Rabbits have a unique digestive system: Rabbits have a unique digestive system that allows them to extract nutrients from their food more efficiently.

Snake

🐾 Because snakes are reptiles, they breathe air and have scales.

🐾 The world has over 3,000 species of snakes.

🐾 Snakes have translucent scales covering their eyes rather than eyelids.

🐾 Snakes typically begin to eat by swallowing their prey's head entirely.

🐾 Snakes can detect heat, which helps them find warm-blooded prey.

🐾 Snakes can survive without food for months.

- Snakes can be found everywhere but Antarctica.

- Venomous snakes use their fangs to inject venom into their victim.

- The majority of snakes are harmless to people and non-venomous.

- Snakes cannot blink because they lack eyelids!

- As snakes are unable to bite, they must strangle and then swallow food whole.

- Some snakes can pass through a wedding band because they are so tiny!

- Snakes' tongues can detect smells.

- A few snake species can scale trees.

- A few snakes have wings! They move between trees via gliding.

- Snakes may spend up to two hours submerged!

- The Black Mamba, which can move up to 12.5 miles per hour, is the fastest snake in the world.

- A nest or bed refers to a collection of snakes.

- Snakes have a unique way of reproducing: Most snake species reproduce by laying eggs, but some species give birth to live young.

- Snakes shed their skin, they do this as they grow. The process is called molting and happens several times a year.

- Snakes move in an unusual manner known as "undulation" because they propel themselves ahead by tightening and relaxing their muscles.

Tiger

- **Tigers, the largest species of cat, are now only found in Asia, but they were once also widespread in Africa and Europe.**

- **Tigers can blend in with their surroundings thanks to the unique stripes on their coats.**

- **Tigers only consume meat since they are carnivores.**

- **The majority of tigers hunt small animals like deer and wild pigs in forests or grasslands.**

- **Around 3,900 tigers remain in the world today.**

- 🐾 Tigers can swim at a speed of 6 miles per hour and run at 35 miles per hour.

- 🐾 In the wild, tigers can live up to 26 years.

- 🐾 Tigers are capable of 10-meter leaps.

- 🐾 Tigers are solitary creatures who typically live by themselves.

- 🐾 Tigers are the national animals of South Korea, Malaysia, Bangladesh, and India.

- 🐾 Each tigers stripes are unique like a fingerprint.

- 🐾 To demarcate their area, tigers enjoy roaring loudly.

- 🐾 Tigers are capable of 16-foot vertical jumps.

- 🐾 Tiger cubs weigh only a few pounds and are born blind.

- 🐾 For thousands of years, tigers have served as metaphors for power and strength.

- 🐾 Tigers may hear sounds that are too high or low for people to hear since they have a keen sense of hearing.

- With males weighing up to 600 pounds and females up to 400 pounds, tigers are the biggest of the great cats.

- Because of their great swimming abilities, tigers enjoy being in the water. In search of prey, they are known to swim across lakes and rivers.

- Tigers have excellent night vision.

Urchin

🐾 Marine invertebrates called sea urchins have hard, spiky shells.

🐾 Sea urchins come in over 950 different species.

🐾 Sea urchins are present in every ocean in the globe, ranging in depth from the intertidal zone to more than 7,000 meters.

🐾 Sea urchins are significant grazers in the ocean and assist in controlling algae.

🐾 To aid in movement, sea urchins have five double rows of tube feet.

🐾 To remove algae from rocks, sea urchins have a particular jaw known as Aristotle's lantern.

- Sea urchins have an unusual reproductive mechanism in which both sexes simultaneously release their eggs and sperm into the ocean.

- Marine life including starfish and sea otters enjoy eating sea urchins.

- Sea urchins have a 30-year lifespan.

- Sea urchins play a significant role in the ocean food chain and contribute to the ocean's overall health.

- There are more than 200 spines on a sea urchin's body.

- Sand dollars and starfish are relatives of sea urchins.

- To eat their meal, sea urchins use their five teeth.

- To move, sea urchins can roll themselves into a ball.

- Kelp, algae, and other small invertebrates are consumed by sea urchins.

- Sea urchins can endure down to 6,500 feet in depth.

- There have been sea urchins on the planet for 350 million years.

- Sea urchins have the ability to alter their color to blend in.

- Sea urchins are incapable of swimming; instead, they merely float in the currents.

Vulture

🐾 **Vultures are large scavenging birds of prey, with bald heads, long wings, and hooked beaks.**

🐾 **There are 23 species of vultures in the world, which can be found in Africa, Eurasia, and North and South America.**

🐾 **Vultures mainly feed on carrion, the remains of dead animals.**

🐾 **Vultures are important scavengers in our ecosystems as they keep the environment clean by removing dead animals and preventing the spread of disease.**

- Vultures have an incredibly strong sense of smell, which helps them locate food from miles away.

- Certain species of vultures have a wingspan that can reach three meters and are also able to soar for extended periods of time.

- In the wild, vultures can live for up to 40 years.

- Vultures play a crucial role in maintaining the balance of species in the habitats they live in.

- In several regions of the world, vultures are subject to severe persecution and hunting, endangering their future.

- In many nations, vultures are legally protected, and conservation measures are in progress to help safeguard them.

- As vultures lack teeth, they eat entirely by swallowing their food.

- Vultures typically discover their prey already dead, thus they don't need to go hunting for food

- Because of their keen vision, vultures can locate a dead animal from great distances.

- Instead of using their wings for flight, vultures utilize them to soar through the air currents.

- Several vulture species, like the Turkish Vulture, have a defense mechanism where they can hurl vomit to ward off predators.

- Because they consume carrion, vultures are known to have extremely acidic stomachs that may dissolve bacteria and poisons, protecting them from diseases that would kill other animals.

- When it's hot out, vultures have a special method of cooling off. They will urinate on their legs, which lowers their body temperature as the urine evaporates.

- When feasting on a carcass, vultures can be seen in vast flocks, known as a wake.

Wolf

🐾 Because they hunt and live in groups, wolves are social animals.

🐾 Except for Antarctica, all continents are home to wolves.

🐾 In the wild, wolves can live up to 13 years, while in captivity, they can live for up to 25 years.

🐾 Wolves use a variety of sounds, body language cues, and scent markings to communicate with one another.

🐾 Moose, elk, and deer are among the large species that wolves, which are carnivores, prey on.

- Wolves are apex predators, which means they are at the top of the food chain.

- Wolves have thick fur and bushy tails that help keep them warm in cold weather.

- All domestic dogs have wolves as their ancestors.

- The grey wolf, which may reach up to 175 pounds, is the largest wolf species.

- Wolves have a complex social hierarchy within their packs, with each wolf having a specific rank and role.

- Wolves have a unique vocal repertoire that consists of howls, whines, growls, and barks.

- Wolves dislike being around people. They feel more at ease in the outdoors.

- Wolves are capable of running at speeds up to 35 mph, which is quicker than a cheetah!

- Wolves are capable of 10-foot vertical jumps.

- Wolves have an acute sense of smell that is up to 100 times more acute than that of a human.

🐾 Wolves have eyes that shine in the dark and can see in it.

🐾 Wolves frequently look out for one another and travel in packs.

🐾 Wolves are incredibly intelligent and are capable of opening doors and cages.

🐾 Wolves howl to let other wolves know where they are and to communicate with one another.

🐾 Wolves have been observed to mimic the sound of a human infant crying in an effort to draw prey to them.

X-ray fish

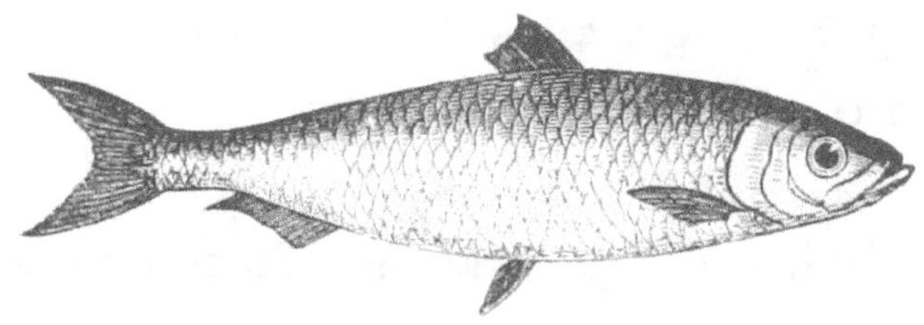

- X-ray fish, also known as "Pristella maxillaris," are indigenous to South America's Amazon and Orinoco rivers.

- They have long thin bodies with silver patches, and a base color that ranges from yellow to gold.

- X-ray fish have a maximum length of 4 cm and a maximum lifespan of 5 years.

- Being an omnivorous animal, they will consume the majority of live, frozen, and flake foods.

- They live in a heated aquarium of at least 10 gallons and are best kept in groups of five or more.

- X-ray fish enjoy swimming around in their aquariums and are quite active.

- They get along well with other fish in their tank and are a fairly calm species.

- X-ray fish lay eggs, and they do so on the tank's plants and other surfaces.

- Because X-ray fish are sensitive to the quality of the water, the tank must be kept clean and in good condition.

- X-ray fish are an excellent choice for novice fish keepers because they are reasonably simple to care for.

- To evade predators, X-ray fish can alter their transparency.

- In the 1980s, X-ray fish were found in South America.

- X-ray fish have a maximum jump height of 3 feet.

- X-ray fish have a top speed of 6 mph.

- The translucent scales and organs of X-ray fish allow you to actually view their "skeleton."

- The unique organ in X-ray fish's heads aids in the detection of their prey.

- X-ray fish can survive in captivity for up to five years.

- X-ray fish have the ability to alter their color to better fit their environment.

- The scales and organs of X-ray fish can emit light.

Yak

🐾 Yaks are sizable creatures that can be found in Asia's Himalayan mountains.

🐾 While Yaks are considerably larger and with thicker, longer fur than cattle, they are linked.

🐾 Yaks can grow to a height of 6 feet and a weight of 1,500 pounds.

🐾 Yaks have curved horns that can grow up to two feet in length.

🐾 Although they can be white or grey, yaks are often black or brown.

- Yaks are practical animals because they can tow carts, plow fields, and carry huge loads.

- Yaks may also produce meat, fleece, and milk.

- In the summer, yaks shave off their heavy winter coats.

- Yaks dwell in herds of up to 20 other yaks and are gregarious creatures.

- Yaks are an endangered species, and overgrazing and climate change are reducing their population.

- Yaks are large, thick-coated creatures with shaggy coats that assist keep them warm in the chilly Himalayan regions.

- The fur on yaks has two layers: a rough outer layer and a soft inner one.

- Grass, leaves, and shrubs are all things yaks adore eating.

- Yaks are highly sturdy and can lift up to 150 pounds of weight!

 Yaks have a top speed of 25 mph!

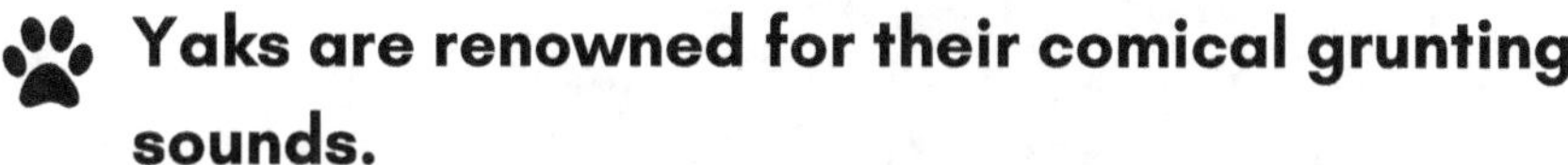 Yaks are renowned for their comical grunting sounds.

Yaks have a maximum lifespan of 20 years in the wild and 40 years in captivity.

Yaks can jump higher than three feet!

Zebra

🐾 Grasslands and savannas are the main habitats of zebras in Africa.

🐾 Horses and donkeys are related to zebras.

🐾 Zebras have white and black striped coats to help them blend in.

🐾 Zebras are protected from the sun and predators by their thick coats.

🐾 Zebras are capable of running at up to 40 mph.

🐾 How wonderful is it that a bunch of zebras is referred to as a "dazzle"?

🐾 Each zebra is distinguished by a certain pattern of stripes.

- Each zebra is distinguished by a certain pattern of stripes.

- Zebras are extremely gregarious creatures that frequently coexist in big groups.

- Zebras tear branches off trees and dig for roots with their hooves.

- Zebras have a 25-year lifespan in the wild.

- Zebras are black and white, but no two have the same stripes; they are all distinct, just like a person's fingerprint.

- Zebras consume grass, twigs, leaves, fruit, and bark.

- Zebras sleep standing up, and they frequently alternate between watching for predators and sleeping while the rest of the herd snoozes.

- After a few hours of birth, baby zebras, known as foals, can stand and run.

- Zebras are capable swimmers but like to stay out of deep water.

- Zebras can produce a wide range of noises and have great hearing.

- Predators like lions, hyenas, and wild dogs have been seen to be kicked by zebras using their hooves.

- Zebras, despite looking like horses, are not tamed animals and are notoriously challenging to train. When confronted, they have a powerful fight-or-flight response and can become unpredictable and violent.

- In order to listen for predators, they also have enormous ears that can rotate independently.

9 781916 791039